THE
INNOVATION
IMPERATIVE

THE
INNOVATION IMPERATIVE

A Business Fable that takes you
on a Journey of Innovation

RANGA SHETTY and SAJITHRA K

Notion Press

Old No. 38, New No. 6
McNichols Road, Chetpet
Chennai - 600 031

First Published by Notion Press 2017
Copyright © Ranga Shetty and Sajithra K 2017
All Rights Reserved.

ISBN 978-1-946436-41-2

This book has been published with all efforts taken to make the material error-free after the consent of the author. However, the author and the publisher do not assume and hereby disclaim any liability to any party for any loss, damage, or disruption caused by errors or omissions, whether such errors or omissions result from negligence, accident, or any other cause.

No part of this book may be used, reproduced in any manner whatsoever without written permission from the author, except in the case of brief quotations embodied in critical articles and reviews.

Scanning QR codes is simple if you have the following:-

- A QR code to scan
- A smart phone
- An application on your phone that is a QR code reader

We have a QR code for you hidden in the four leaf clover. If your smart phone is not preloaded with a reader, here is a list of QR code readers to get you started!

Top 10 free QR code scanners for iPhone and Android
1. INIGMA
2. ZAPPER
3. QR CODE READER BY SCAN
4. KASPERSKY QR SCANNER
5. QUICK SCAN – QR CODE READER
6. QR READER FOR IPHONE/ANDROID
7. QR CODE READER AND SCANNER BY SHOPSAVVY
8. NEO READER
9. QR DROID
10. TAP MEDIA's QR READER

Contents

Preface ix

Chapter 1	Luck by Design	1
Chapter 2	Big Leap!	17
Chapter 3	The Overnight Innovator	31
Chapter 4	Knowing What You Don't Know	39
Chapter 5	Facing Facts	49
Chapter 6	Failing Fast	57
Chapter 7	Kintsukuroi	65
Chapter 8	Vortex	75

Appendix 87

About the Authors 91

Preface

From Ranga Shetty's pen:

In 1991 one of my professors at management school mentioned a book, The Goal by Eli Goldratt. This book captured my imagination. If you haven't read it, here is a synopsis from the cover flap - *"Alex Rogo is a harried plant manager working ever more desperately to try improve performance. His factory is rapidly heading for disaster. So is his marriage. He has ninety days to save his plant - or it will be closed by corporate HQ, with hundreds of job losses. It takes a chance meeting with a professor from student days - Jonah - to help him break out of conventional ways of thinking to see what needs to be done."* The objective of this book is to explain the Theory of Constraints, a concept developed by the author, Eli. The idea of using a story to explain a complex theory created a deep impression on me. It is now over two and a half decades since I first read this book and I still draw inspiration from it. Sajithra and I have borrowed Eli's story-telling style in this first book of ours.

Our book is an attempt to address an emerging need in the talent marketplace. William Gibson, a science fiction writer believes that "The future is already here - it is just not very evenly distributed." If you are a knowledge worker and are wondering how to optimally position yourself in the talent marketplace of the future, this book is for you.

I am sure you have all heard of the 18th century being called as the Agricultural Age, the 19th century as the Industrial Age and the 20th century as the Information Age. What kind of age is the 21st century? Daniel Pink, the best-selling author of several books on business and management, calls this the Conceptual Age. In the Information Age, technical skills were the keys to success. Knowledge workers applied their technical skills to digitize, automate, optimize and remote-enable work. The Conceptual Age is all about bringing new ideas to life. Mere technical skills are not enough. It is not about how much you know. It is about what value you can create and deliver with the skills and knowledge that you have. To be successful you will need to think creatively, test and validate hypotheses rapidly, connect the dots between the idea and its ecosystem and socialize your ideas with authenticity. This book shows you how you can prepare yourself for the Conceptual Age.

The concepts presented in this book are not my own discoveries or inventions. I came across them at different times in different sources during my endeavours to continuously expand my horizons. They have helped me along in my professional journey as I connected with amazing teams and delivered innovative products. When I decided to write this book, I started to assemble these concepts and they very naturally fell into place in this simple four-legged framework that I now call the Four Disciplines of Innovation.

This book is the culmination of extraordinary influences on my life, most of all from my parents who were instrumental in instilling in me this undying urge to expand my horizons and from my wife who constantly reminds me that the only way to live a life less ordinary is by getting out of your comfort zone.

Finally, this book is for Ashwin, Shivani and Saumya - you know what you mean to me.

From Sajithra's pen

'Innovation' is the most pervasively used term in the Industry today, and understandably so. Innovation is not only about accolades and laurels; it is about survival. Innovation is the quintessential linchpin that determines if a company's next stop is up the mountain or down the valley. The stakes have never been higher!

The first blueprint of this book was Ranga's scribbled notes on a couple of loose sheets. This later took the form of a fable of our protagonist Kumar's Innovation journey with his mentor Judith. Every smart engineer we have ever met lent something that has made the character Kumar come alive. We attempted to break down the Innovation process to design an easy Roadmap for Kumar. This Innovation Roadmap can help anyone with a will to pursue Innovation. Kumar's journey can be yours too.

'Innovation' is often confused with 'Invention' and that can be unfair. It makes people wary of using the term 'Innovation' or identifying themselves as an 'Innovator'. Invention refers to creating an original concept or product. Innovation is about finding the right use for a product - existing or original. Innovators do not necessarily invent a product but they always manage to find a good use for one. And, they venture out to create a new world in ways - big and small.

If we are asked to trace the origin of our civilization to a single point, it's easy to start from the discovery of fire. Finding different uses of fire set us on a trajectory of evolution that made us who we are today. Apparently, eating cooked meat shrunk the digestive tract, allowing more energy to the growing brain of homo erectus. Extending the time of work with lanterns at night allowed them to create new things - such as tools. The Stone Age gave way to Bronze Age. The world changed. Only the Homo Sapiens survived, leaving behind the Neanderthals.

No one knows exactly why the Neanderthals became extinct when the Homo Sapiens survived. They both had access to 'fire'. Many scientists attribute this to adaptability to new ambiguous conditions like climate changes. How they used fire determined their survival. When a new variable is at play, adapting to that with novel application of ideas is Innovation. It's not merely about what you have. What you do with what you have matters more.

Imagine for a moment being transported to that time period. What do you see? There is scientific evidence that both Neanderthals and Homo Sapiens used fire to cook their food. And, most of them lived in Eurasia at the time. They both battled similar conditions. Harsh, cold weather. Unpredictable animal attacks. Food scarcity. Is it possible that a single person determined the survival of Homo Saphiens? Did a Homo Sapien offer a suggestion that fire could be controlled inside their caves to keep them warm? This is admittedly an ambiguous scenario. No one had used fire inside a cave till then. What this person could have done next to validate that idea, convince others, and ultimately ensure the survival of their species? Reading this book will answer that question in the context of a Knowledge worker.

We are at the crossroads where the much-revered Information Age is evolving out. Mid and Senior professionals in the Tech Industry are facing the brunt of it. At work, they face "bigger" challenges which typically imply more ambiguity, more impact to business outcomes, more risk etc. If you are a knowledge professional looking for a Roadmap to navigate such troubled waters, this book is for you. If you are a senior leader looking for a simple teaching tool for your team, this book will help you do just that. And, if you are a fresher who questions the status quo or a student who wants to change the world, take a bow. This book is for you!

To

Castiel San-Saj and Seraphim San-Saj – *You came into our lives on the day of Magna Carta and true to that, you changed our lives forever. Here's hoping that you work hard to become the best that you can be and have fun while you are at it.*

Sanju Sebastian, *the San part of San-Saj for also being its sane part.*

My Parents, *for defying all cultural norms to encourage my freedom.*

Chapter 1
Luck by Design

Luck is the residue of design

-Branch Rickey

"Sorry Sir. Your card is invalid!"

"**Sir!** Please check if the card is past its expiry date."

The barista in the airport cafe wondered for a split second why the man froze at a simple request but she had other things to worry about. Her days were about serving long queues of caffeine starved people, and sending them away, only to see more added in their stead. After a while, all her customers looked the same, no different than a chipmunk on a wheel.

He quickly presented another card and got back to his seat with a Cafe Frappé.

Kumar had lately been feeling like a cog in a wheel, the important piece that mostly gets ignored and sometimes lost in the magnanimity of the big picture. Like many middle-class children in India, he graduated with good grades from a NIT college and joined a MNC. Life followed a predictable pattern with a car EMI and week end trips with friends. That pattern changed a year back when he accepted the job as a Lead Engineer at EZroads, a hot Silicon Valley start-up.

EZroads was valued at $5 Billion at the end of its second year. And, when they launched a Product Innovation Centre in Bangalore, the tech landscape in India embraced it into its fold with much fanfare. Kumar's family, true to its middle-class roots didn't share that enthusiasm. His father, a retired bank officer was highly suspicious of their huge valuation. It's all a bubble he told him for what could literally be the hundredth time.

Kumar took up the role, much to the surprise of his family. Indian households didn't work that way. Elders in the family usually had the final say. He joined the company with a substantial hike in salary. Everything was forgiven and forgotten when he announced that he had booked an apartment. Indian households seemed to work that way. Glittering milestones outshine obedience. And shine, he did!

EZroads was launched by two friends who graduated from Stanford in the Silicon Valley. Meredith Scully, an Irish American and Rahul Patel, a second-generation Indian American. Avid hikers, they built an app that helps in planning road trips. The app was called "Road Trip Genie." The idea was for the app to be the genie that serves users an incredible travel experience. The app combined a specialized search engine with social networking functionality.

This allowed users to search relevant content, interact with their social network for inputs, and pull together a trip plan, all with a few clicks on their smartphone app. The app garnered millions of users within months. Word got around and it didn't take long for the VCs to pump their money in, to become part of their success story.

The India centre was structured into two divisions - Search and Social. Each division had a Director, a Product Manager, a Lead Engineer, and about 15 Engineers. Kumar joined the 'Social' division, as its Lead Engineer, a year back. He built up the team and took over the code base from the US engineers that had written the original code. As soon as they got the code base, he put in place a rigorous process for ensuring high quality standards were met for any changes and additions to the code. His initiative to build a very effective partnership with Aman Sharma, the Product Manager enabled them to rapidly turnaround new requirements into production ready features in the product. The Social division in Bangalore was rapidly developing a solid reputation for its tech prowess.

His Annual Appraisal was a month away when the Division's Director called him and Aman for a meeting.

"I am sorry. I have bad news for you guys. Yesterday we reviewed the customer usage report at the CTO Staff meeting" He pursed his lips, let out a sigh and continued "The report revealed some serious problems with the social features in Road Trip Genie.

Our division is now being considered as the weak link in the product."

Aman stopped him. He wasn't buying it.

"What? We work the hardest in the company. We have built a competent team, the best in the Industry. Everything is done by the book. How can we possibly be the weak link? Who says this?"

"The users, Aman. There are too many users dropping out of the app while using the social features."

"But that's not possible," Kumar countered, a worried frown creasing his forehead. "This must be some misunderstanding. I have reviewed the production logs. There are no signs of any application failures in any of the social features. In fact, our production support team has rated the social features as the most robust functionality in the whole product."

"Kumar, I know you and your team have done a phenomenal job with the code. I have always vouched for the quality of the code produced by your team. And for what it's worth, I too was surprised by the data in the report. Be that as it may, the user dropout rate is getting a lot of attention. Our investor called the CTO to ask about this and warned him that this could mean that the next round of investment is in question."

Kumar felt his pulse rise. His words tumbled out faster and faster.

"I don't understand. How can the best piece of code in the product be the problem? Aman will also attest to the fact that we have implemented all the features laid out in the requirements document with a very elegant design. Some of the search features on the other hand are just hacks. Everyone knows that their code quality cannot hold a candle to ours."

The Director paused for a second. He was getting late for his next meeting.

"Kumar, technical excellence is not enough. Let me jog your memory. Six months ago, when we last discussed your team's performance appraisal, I asked you to develop more of a product mindset in your team. Strong software engineering discipline is necessary but not sufficient to succeed in a product company. Aman is responsible for working with the market-facing teams in the US to figure out the feature set. However, I expect you to contribute value on this front as well. You should understand how your components fit into the big picture and deliver value to the customer. There is clearly a miss here. We are not delivering value to the customer. Hence the bad dropout rate. I need you to step up and think innovatively. We cannot lose any more time on this. We have a month to come up with a solution and present it to the CTO. Aman has a personal situation and will not be able to travel. I would need you to travel to the US and make the presentation to the CTO."

Kumar couldn't process anything beyond the thought that his team, which was arguably the best engineering team in the company, were not the super heroes anymore.

He walked out the door, mumbling to himself "Technical excellence is not enough? We are not delivering value to the customer. I thought I was doing a phenomenal job as an engineering lead. I am being asked to step up...?"

The next month passed them by in a blur. Kumar and Aman had come up with a proposed solution to the user dropout problem.

Today, Kumar was on his way to San Francisco to present the solution to the CTO and the Marketing team. However, the Director's comments were still nagging Kumar. The words "not delivering value" and "need you to step up" kept ringing in his ears. Would the proposed solution solve the problem? He wasn't very sure. Was his job on the line too? For the first time in his career he felt like an underachiever. What was he missing? His Director had asked him to "think innovatively." What did that mean? How do you innovate? Was the new proposed solution innovative? Other clichéd terms like "think out of the box" and "design thinking" flickered through his mind. But no one had ever explained to him how he was supposed to do those things. All his past performance appraisals proved irrevocably that he was a very good software engineer. Now it appeared that he was expected to be much more than that. He was expected to innovate. Is that a skill that he wasn't gifted with? How could he transform from a 'very good software engineer' to an 'Innovator'?

This is an announcement for passengers on flight 132 to SFO. The flight has been delayed by 3 hours due to bad weather conditions. We now expect to board at 11:30 PM

Kumar scanned the waiting area near the departure gate. It was going to get crowded soon, given the delayed departure of his flight. He found a quiet corner far away from the walkways and snack counters. He just didn't feel like making idle conversation with strangers who were going to be thrown together into cramped spaces for hours.

A few minutes later, a woman in her late 50s approached his corner and occupied the seat next to him. She had one of those faces that begets smiles as a reflex.

"Hi. I am Judith Holtz. Lovely to meet you"

"Hi Ms. Holtz. I am Kumar. The flight is delayed by 3 hours and here we are, an hour early. What a waste of time."

Kumar did not know that Judith was also in the same queue in the Cafe. She had noticed how absent-minded he was during his encounter with the barista.

"Time is precious, Kumar. It is up to us to not let it go to waste. Where are you headed?

"I am going to San Francisco for a meeting with my CTO."

Kumar wondered if his response came across as boasting. But Judith just continued the conversation "Which company do you work for?"

'EZroads' said Kumar. Judith didn't look like someone from the tech industry. He did not expect her to recognize the company name.

"Oh! You are the guys behind Road Trip Genie. My son Steve was telling me about your app the other day. He is an avid biker and is always looking for new destinations for his biking trips. He believes that you guys have hit upon a splendid market opportunity."

Kumar could not help giving in to a feeling of pride. Judith surely knew that his company was an up and coming unicorn.

Then Judith said something that plunged him down to earth. "I hope you don't mind my saying this. But Steve stopped using your app after a few months. He felt that your product's social features need improvement. Even though your app enabled him to discover many new destinations, he said that he was not able to get much help from the social features in Road Trip Genie."

That comment jolted through him like a punch. Without realizing it, Kumar became very defensive. "How many friends does Steve have in his online social network? Maybe his network is very small and hence Road Trip Genie couldn't find much relevant social content for him."

Judith was taken aback by his reaction but she also realized that this meant he was opening up.

"Oh, I am sorry. I can't explain why he did not find the social features very useful. I am not much of a social networker on the Internet. I am too old for that I guess. I prefer social networking in person, over coffee or lunch. I am sure your company has its best minds working on this problem."

At that moment, Kumar didn't believe that Judith could help him. But that didn't stop him from pouring his heart out. He introduced himself as the Lead engineer who owned the social features of Road Trip Genie and told her that he owned responsibility for solving the problem that her son had faced with the product. He also explained that he and his product manager had come up with a proposed solution, but were not confident that it would address the problem.

"Why do you think your proposed solution may not address the problem?" Judith asked, sliding past the fact that he had just acknowledged that the product had a problem.

That was an easy question for Kumar to answer. "The problem is not with the design or quality of the software. If it was one of those kinds of problems, I would have a fix in no time. We don't quite know why users are dropping out after trying out the social features. Our guess is that users are not getting enough social content and so we have widened the scope to the user's 3rd degree connections. I don't like these kinds of problems where I must rely upon guesswork. I am going to be uncomfortable presenting this proposed solution to the CTO. I am still struggling to come up with a logical explanation for how the proposed solution will address our problem."

Judith noticed that Kumar was quite agitated with his dilemma. She empathized with him. "Ah! I understand now. You are thinking like a good engineer. You are looking for a clear logical solution that you can derive from a diligent analysis of the problem."

Kumar wasn't done being agitated yet. He carried on, "My boss may not agree with you about me being a good engineer. His comment to me was that technical excellence is not enough. I need to innovate if I want to win his approval. Unfortunately, there is no formula or algorithm for innovation. I can't just dream up an innovative solution, especially for a problem as vague as this."

Judith was listening intently. She knew that she could help him but he needed to relax first and not feel compelled to be defensive. "Kumar, you are a lead engineer at an up and coming unicorn. They trust you enough to give you ownership of a key component of their product. You must be a good engineer. I know that EZroads has a very rigorous selection process. I am sure you have excellent credentials. Tell me if I am wrong."

Kumar thought for a moment and then replied, "I have been a top performer throughout my career. It wasn't easy. I am the first engineer in my whole extended family. I have a passion for technology and my parents supported and nurtured my ambition whole-heartedly. I have put my heart and soul into becoming the best engineer I can be. Neither my efforts nor my results have ever fallen short of expectations until now. But now, I just don't know how to produce a winning solution. Innovation is a game of chance. If I am lucky, my solution will click with customers. Else it will be in the trash can in the next release. I just wish there was a more defined approach to innovation."

Judith recognized the crisis that Kumar was dealing with. Here was a good engineer who had successfully learnt how to apply advanced technical skills to well-defined requirements and problems. He had practiced his trade with perfection. However, he was now struggling with a problem that was not well-defined. She decided then that she would offer him her guidance. After all, with the delayed flight and the long layover on her way home to San Francisco, she had a lot of time on her hands and wanted to put it to good use. She had to first get Kumar to change his mindset about innovation.

"You can actually have a structured approach to innovation. It's not all a game of chance as you imagine it to be," she said.

"There are several one hit wonders in the tech world. And that is why many people think that innovation is a game of chance. But then there are people who have produced a series of innovations over long periods of time. It can't just be luck. I am sure you know Thomas Alva Edison invented the electric light bulb, the phonograph, the motion picture camera and many other useful innovations. He was either one lucky guy or maybe he figured out a successful approach to guide his innovative endeavours. I prefer to believe the latter."

Judith continued, "I retired 5 years ago from a tech company. I have had the good fortune of working with many good engineers during the course of my career. Some of them can consistently attack ambiguous problems, produce extra-ordinary ideas and nurture them into impactful solutions. They are rock stars. They are the true innovators. I have watched them closely. Their thought processes and techniques can be learnt and practiced by any good engineer."

Kumar was intrigued. As far as first impressions go, he found Judith wise and compassionate but he didn't really expect her to be able to help him with his complex problem. Maybe he was wrong. If she has worked with rock star innovators, he might be able to learn some techniques that he might apply to his problem.

"I am sorry. I didn't take you to be the techie type, Ms. Holtz. May I ask where you worked?"

"Oh. I am one of the founders of Infodex."

Judith did not want to talk too much about herself. Kumar was too overwhelmed by his own problem to be interested in anything else and he didn't ask her any more personal questions. He did vaguely remember an article about one of the founders of Infodex, a billionaire joining the 'Giving Pledge', a campaign by Warren Buffett and Bill Gates with the goal to encourage the wealthy people of the world to give most their net worth to philanthropy. Today he was more interested in understanding how a good engineer can become a rock star innovator.

Infodex has branches in major cities all over the world. Working across cultures and countries, Judith found that the main challenges remained the same though the specific details varied. All good professionals go through three inflection points in their career. The first is when they transition from academia to industry. This is when they should figure out how to apply their skills to real-world problems. Kumar certainly had handled this inflection point very well and thus had launched his career into a high growth trajectory. It was the second inflection point that he was having trouble with.

Professionals who are very good at what they do, are measured by a different yardstick. They are expected to take on "bigger" challenges which typically implies more ambiguity, more impact to business outcomes, more risk, etc. In short they are measured on their ability to innovate. This is the second inflection point and this is where Kumar was stuck.

After her retirement, Judith had maintained her connection with the company by conducting regular workshops on innovation. She was on her way back to San Francisco from one of those workshops in Bangalore. Judith was helping the company executives with the third inflection point which involves the transition from an "innovator" to a "force-multiplier."

The third inflection point is far in the future for Kumar. For now, Judith had to help him with figuring out how to become an innovator.

Judith clearly was eminently qualified to help Kumar with his second inflection point. She had coached many others like Kumar.

Kumar too was eager to learn from Judith's experience. He asked her, "Can there really be a structured approach to innovation? Isn't innovation by its very definition truly unique and therefore unpredictable? A structured approach means that it is repeatable and predictable. How can a repeatable and predictable process produce a unique outcome?"

"Excellent question," said Judith. "You are right in that following a single line of thinking repeatedly and predictably will not generate new ideas for your innovations. You will need to think differently. Most people approach a problem or requirement in a certain way based on their training, their cultural biases, their strengths and weakness, etc. They need to be forced to think differently. You could have a structured approach that forces you to explore alternative lines of thought. But that's not all. Another important point to note is that the implementation of a unique idea is just an invention. For it to become an innovation you have to figure out a way for someone to derive significant value from the invention. The path from invention to innovation is riddled with potholes. Some inventions will not survive this path; others will need to be tweaked and modified before they deliver the promised value. You can follow a structured approach to traverse this path."

This was starting to make sense to Kumar. His agitation was giving way to a feeling of hope and excitement. He really wanted to learn more. There was a lot he could learn from Judith and who knows he may even be able to come up with a cool innovative solution that could wow his CTO.

"Judith, you have got to teach me this structured approach."

Fun Exercise:

One of the greatest advances in medicine is the discovery of Penicillin which began the era of antibiotics. Sir Alexander Fleming is credited with the discovery of Penicillin in 1928. As the story goes, Fleming returned from a two-week vacation and noticed that a mold had developed on an accidently contaminated staphylococcus culture plate. This mold, Penicillium Notatum, appeared to have prevented the growth of staphylococci which led him to conclude that something in this mold was a bacteria killer. It was fourteen years later, in March 1942 that the first patient was successfully treated with Penicillin.

Try and guess why it took 14 years for Penicillin to become a successful drug?

Chapter 2
Big Leap!

Life is a travelling to the edge of knowledge, then a leap taken

-D. H. Lawrence

Thud!

Judith and Kumar stopped talking. A kid, goofing around, had walked into an unmarked glass door. He was now crying loudly. The parents scooped the kid up and carried him to the lounge area. Kumar didn't know how to react. He looked around to see people giving this incident a moment's attention, only to get back to what they were doing. Not Judith! She leafed through her folder and found a bunch of Post-it notes, all the while walking towards that glass door. Then, she scribbled something on a Post-it note and stuck it on the door. 'Problem solved!', Kumar thought.

The Post-it note would serve as a stand-in solution till the airport authorities find a permanent one. She got back to her seat and continued the conversation without missing a beat.

"Kumar, yes I can teach you the structured approach. Do you know the story of how the Post-it note was invented? Let me tell you the story before we start our lesson."

Kumar sat straight like an eager student in the classroom of his favourite teacher and nodded, beaming.

Judith liked telling stories. They always made the lessons more memorable. Today, the Post-it notes story would be a perfect opening for her lesson on how to embrace ambiguity.

"I was in school when my father shared something with me that completely changed my outlook on problems and solutions. He was working in 3M at the time. His colleague Spencer Silver set out to create a super strong adhesive but he ended up with one of the weakest adhesives ever produced in 3M. The product was shelved since it did not come anywhere close to meeting the objective of a good adhesive. It remained on the shelf for 6 years.

That was when another colleague, Arthur Fry was dealing with a common problem that many of us have faced. He was frustrated with the bookmarks in his hymn book that kept falling out, making him lose track. He was looking for a bookmark that stuck to the page when he needed it to and could be removed when he needed to move it to a different page. He re-imagined the bookmark as a small piece of paper with a mild adhesive on one side. He had heard about Spencer's weak adhesive. Call it an educated guess or a leap-of-faith. He decided to pick up where Spencer had left off and thus went on to invent the Post-it note."

Kumar was intrigued. "So the legendary Post-it note was born because of Spencer accidentally inventing a weak adhesive. Isn't that just luck? I thought you didn't believe in luck as a primary source of innovation," he asked mischievously.

Judith smiled. "You are right. The weak adhesive was invented by accident. However, that invention stayed on the shelf for 6 years. It did not become an innovative product until Arthur Fry took it up. Let's try and dissect how Arthur went about solving his problem. He needed a way to keep the bookmark attached to a page temporarily. He also needed to be able to detach the bookmark from the page when he needed to move it. I remember using paper clips to hold my bookmarks in place. I am sure many others would have come up with that solution. Remember this was a time when adhesives were only used to permanently stick one thing to another. Until then no had ever thought of using adhesives as a "temporary glue." Arthur could imagine the concept of a temporary glue. This seems to be obvious now, in hindsight. However, it was certainly a leap of faith on his part to extend the failed idea of a weak adhesive to a unique new concept of a temporary glue."

"Ok. I buy that," Kumar replied. "But then how does one take a leap of faith and come up with unique ideas like that? Can anyone do it or does your brain have to be wired differently to be that creative?"

Judith could see that Kumar needed clear, logical explanations for everything. Every little detail had to fall in place. Else he would not be satisfied with the explanation. This was typical of people whose natural inclination was to use deductive reasoning over other forms. She was sure that Kumar hadn't even considered other reasoning styles when confronted with a problem in the past. She was going to change that.

Judith maintained a calm and patient demeanour, a characteristic acquired through years of mentoring experience. "Kumar, everyone's brains are wired differently. That's why each one of us has our own individual traits. We talk differently, we behave differently, we react differently and so on. The question is 'Do we think and reason differently?'. Over years of training, we learn to adopt a single structured approach to problem solving to make us more efficient at it. For professionals, the deductive style of thinking and reasoning is the most common one that we all adopt. The challenge is to remember that our brain is capable of other alternative styles of thinking and to exercise this diversity of thought when required."

Kumar interjected, "I hope this isn't turning into a philosophical lecture. I have never been interested in philosophy."

"Oh, don't worry. All I am trying to do is to show you that there is an alternative approach to thinking about a problem. Without realizing it, you have been limiting your options by applying the deductive approach exclusively. Thus, you are missing out on all the ideas you could have generated by applying other styles. In particular, I would like to introduce you to the abductive way of thinking." Judith retorted.

She continued, "Do you realize why you are so good at what you do? I can bet you that when you approach a problem, you always rigorously collect all available data and fit them into a mental model of the problem. Once you have them all in place, figuring out the solution is just a matter of applying true and tested principles on the model. This gives you a solution that you can be certain will work. Am I right or am I right?"

"Of course, you are right. That's how a good engineer always delivers on his promise of an optimal working solution. I hope you are not disputing that." Kumar asked.

"Certainly not. But what do you do when the problem is ambiguous, when you don't have a tested mental model of the problem with all the data fitting in nicely?" Judith countered.

Kumar was stumped. He was good at solving complex technical problems. He was the class topper in data structures and algorithms. Throughout his career his software designs were always praised by his peers and his superiors alike. He had not yet encountered a requirement that he couldn't address with an elegant technical design. His mind strayed to some of the complex work he had done over the years. In every instance, he could map the problem to a model that he had learnt about. But now, with Road Trip Genie the problem itself was ambiguous. He couldn't map it to any reference model that he had experience with. And, he suddenly realized why he was so uncomfortable with this problem. He just did not know how to deal with ambiguous problems.

Embarrassed to admit it, he sheepishly said, "Judith, you got me there. I need help with this."

Judith, the patient teacher that she was, very politely replied "Don't worry. It's not that difficult. All you need to understand is that there is an alternative approach. Before we discuss it, let me first emphasize that your approach, the deductive approach, is not a bad one at all. There is a vast body of knowledge that scientists and engineers before us have contributed to over the years. We are trained during our formative years as engineers to leverage this body of knowledge by taking the deductive approach. That's how we stand upon the shoulders of the great engineers who came before us."

Kumar now realized that he was considered a good engineer because he had mastery over the vast body of knowledge in his chosen area of expertise. But then he also realized something else. "If the deductive approach requires proven reference models, it can't help us deal with unsolved problems - ones that cannot be mapped to existing reference models." He did not realize that he had spoken out aloud.

Judith replied, "I couldn't have said it better. This is where the abductive approach comes in. The key difference between the two is that the deductive approach focusses on getting to a correct conclusion, one that you can be certain is correct based on tested and proven principles and models; while as the abductive approach focusses on developing one or more hypotheses that are merely plausible explanations of the problem or may have some possibility of solving it. Our ability to generate new and unique hypotheses is the essence of our creativity."

Kumar interjected, "I can recognize if an explanation or solution is correct or wrong. I am wondering how I recognize if something is *'merely plausible'*."

Judith continued patiently, "This is where you have to get out of your comfort zone. Innovation requires you to get comfortable with not knowing everything. How else will you deal with situations where you have an incomplete set of observations, otherwise known as ambiguous problems? You arrive at the *'merely plausible'* by making educated guesses or leaps of faith. You construct one or more hypotheses based on your educated guesses or leaps of faith."

"Ok, but then the hypotheses could sometimes be wrong even if it is based on your best, most-educated guess," persisted Kumar.

Judith had a ready answer, "Yes, you are right. Abductive thinking is just the first step in creating innovation. This is the ideation stage. Not all your hypotheses will lead to innovations. Only those that successfully go through a process of testing and validation yield viable innovations. But we are jumping ahead. Let's take stock of what you have learnt so far."

Kumar was restless. He wasn't fully satisfied. But he decided to ruminate over what he had learnt so far. "Ok, I will try and be patient. I have more questions. But let me take your advice and work on getting comfortable with not knowing all the answers."

Judith also wanted to put this first lesson into a framework that Kumar could easily use as reference. "So what you have learnt so far is that it is important to be comfortable with ambiguity. One way of dealing with it is by applying abductive thinking which involves constructing hypotheses that lead to plausible solutions. This is the first discipline of innovation. Let's call it 'Embracing Ambiguity'. There are four disciplines in all. We can create a simple picture to help you remember the four disciplines of innovation."

Judith drew a four-leaf clover on a notepad and wrote 'Embracing Ambiguity' on one leaf.

"Do you know that a four-leaf clover is very rare. Three leaf clovers are quite common. Some people believe that finding a four-leaf clover brings good luck. I am not a believer in luck, but I find it fascinating that there is only one four leaf clover for every 10,000 three leaf clovers. I think a four-leaf clover will be a good symbol to represent the four disciplines of innovation. After all innovation is at least as rare as a four-leaf clover, don't you think?"

"Thanks, Judith." Kumar liked the four-leaf clover symbol. But his mind was elsewhere. He was already thinking about his Road Trip Genie problem and wondering how big a leap of faith he would have to make to deliver an innovation.

Good evening, passengers. This is the pre-boarding announcement for flight 132 to SFO....

Kumar wished the flight was delayed by another hour. There was much more he could learn from Judith. He had always thought of ambiguity as a problem to be shunned. His natural inclination was to find the most appropriate model to address the problem and gather all the required data points to populate the model so that there is no ambiguity about the solution. Judith had convinced him that there was another alternative. He needed to get comfortable with 'Embracing Ambiguity'. Would he succeed in finding an innovative solution to his Road Trip Genie problem by embracing ambiguity?

We would like to invite our first- and business-class passengers, and passengers requiring special assistance to board at gate 7.

"Kumar, didn't I tell you that time is precious and that it is up to us to not let it go to waste. We spent the waiting time well, didn't we? This is a perfect break for you to think through our conversation. We can continue our discussion during the layover at Paris."

Fun Exercise:

Stanley Budner's Tolerance of Ambiguity test[1]

Instructions: For each of the statements below, please indicate to what extent the statement is characteristic of you. Please use the following scale and circle the corresponding number:
1 Strongly Disagree 2 Disagree 3 Somewhat Disagree 4 Neither Agree nor Disagree 5 Slightly Agree 6 Somewhat Agree 7 Agree 8 Strongly Agree

1. An expert who doesn't come up with a definite answer probably doesn't know too much

   👎 1-2-3-4-5-6-7-8 🙂

2. I would like to live in a foreign country for a while

   👎 1-2-3-4-5-6-7-8 🙂

3. There is really no such thing as a problem that can't be solved.

   👎 1-2-3-4-5-6-7-8 🙂

4. People who fit their lives to a schedule probably miss most of the joy of living.

   👎 1-2-3-4-5-6-7-8 🙂

---

[1] BUDNER, S. (1962). Intolerance of ambiguity as a personality variable. Journal of Personality, 30(1), 29–50.

5. A good job is one where what is to be done and how it is to be done are always clear.

👎 1-2-3-4-5-6-7-8 😊

6. It is more fun to tackle a complicated problem than to solve a simple one.

👎 1-2-3-4-5-6-7-8 😊

7. In the long run it is possible to get more done by tackling small, simple problems rather than large and complicated ones.

👎 1-2-3-4-5-6-7-8 😊

8. Often the most interesting and stimulating people are those who don't mind being different and original.

👎 1-2-3-4-5-6-7-8 😊

9. What we are used to is always preferable to what is unfamiliar.

👎 1-2-3-4-5-6-7-8 😊

10. People who insist upon a yes or no answer just don't know how complicated things really are.

👎 1-2-3-4-5-6-7-8 😊

11. A person who leads an even, regular life in which few surprises or unexpected happenings arise really has a lot to be grateful for.

👎 1-2-3-4-5-6-7-8 😊

12. Many of our most important decisions are based upon insufficient information.

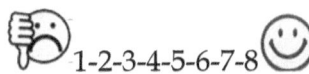 1-2-3-4-5-6-7-8

13. I like parties where I know most of the people more than ones where all or most of the people are complete strangers.

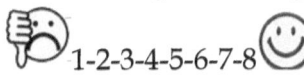 1-2-3-4-5-6-7-8

14. Teachers or supervisors who hand out vague assignments give one a chance to show initiative and originality.

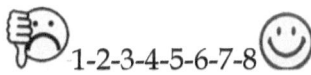 1-2-3-4-5-6-7-8

15. The sooner we all acquire similar values and ideals the better.

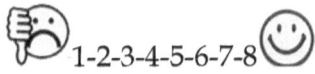 1-2-3-4-5-6-7-8

16. A good teacher is one who makes you wonder about your way of looking at things.

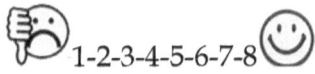 1-2-3-4-5-6-7-8

Chapter 3
The Overnight Innovator

Our overnight success took 1000 days

- Brian Chesky

Kumar sensed the weight of the day drifting away as the flight took off. He had arrived at the airport dejected, expecting the meeting in the San Francisco Office to echo his Director's verdict. 'Step up'. Only, he didn't know how. His conversation with Judith had changed that. Up in the air, he breathed in a glimmer of hope. The seats next to him were not occupied, a welcome relief.

It was late into the night and the flight crew didn't wait long to dim the lights. The passengers settled in to catch a few winks before the next layover. All but Kumar, who opened his laptop to glance through his presentation document.

Problem: Too many users drop out after using the social features of 'Road Trip Genie'.

Context: Road Trip Genie is used for discovering destinations, planning trips and creating travelogues. Its social features enable users to tap into their own social network to assist in the discovery and planning process.

Analysis of the usage logs of these features yielded the following data points -

1. 93% of users use the social features (to broadcast their intent to go on a road trip).
2. The number of first responses to the initial broadcast ranges from 2 to 103.
3. 80% of the cases fall in the band of 10 to 20 first responses.
4. 78% of cases that had conversations of 5 messages or more, continued to plan their trip in the app. Others dropped out.
5. A very small fraction, less than 4%, of the first responses leads to a conversation that runs beyond 5 messages.

Conclusion: A very small percentage of users can generate conversations about their trips that extend beyond 5 messages. Those that succeed in this continue to use the app for planning and documenting their trip.

Proposed Solution: Extend the broadcast of the initial message to second and third degree contacts of the user. This will very likely lead to a larger number of conversations (of 5 messages or more) and thus increase the number of users who will continue to use the app for planning and documenting their trip.

Aman and Kumar had created a simulation of the proposed solution. Using conservative estimates for responses from second and third degree contacts, and assuming that only 4% of initial responses led to longer conversations, they could increase the number of users who stayed with the app to about double the number.

Kumar was uncomfortable with this solution. For one, doubling the number of user retentions from a low base was not a radical improvement. But his discomfort was due to a more fundamental challenge. He needed to understand '*why*' only a small number of initial responses led to a longer conversation. Obviously, only a small number of initial responses appear to have some content that is somehow interesting to the user who was planning the road trip. He had reviewed some of these responses and it was clear from the content of the responses that had generated conversations, that the responder in these cases had useful information that could help with planning of the road trip. Increasing the scope of the initial broadcast would increase the number of responses. But this would not improve the percentage of responses that had useful information. So overall, the proposed solution would increase spam, to both - the user planning the road trip and to his extended social network. This had the potential to further turnoff users.

His deductive analysis had hit a brick wall. Judith was right. He needed to approach this problem differently. He needed a way to increase the percentage of *'useful'* responses. There was no logical solution to this that could guarantee the required result. It was time to practice abductive thinking. He remembered what Judith had said. He needed to construct some hypothesis that would lead to plausible solutions. What was his intuition telling him? He put himself in the role of someone planning a road trip. Who would he reach out to, to get help? Obviously, someone who has made similar road trips or someone who lived in the destination that he planned to visit. How would he identify someone like that? He needed to come up with a hypothesis that enabled him to identify people that had useful information. He racked his brains hard.

Eureka! He had the hypothesis. People who had made similar road trips or lived in the destination that was being considered, had probably uploaded photographs or generated blogs, tweets, Facebook posts, etc. about the trip or the destination. He could identify them by the location code embedded in these kinds of content.

His mind was racing ahead. He knew he was on to something. He wanted to design the solution. But then being the meticulous engineer that he was, he wanted to take the time to document his idea in detail. So, he wrote down -

Hypothesis: People who have uploaded content such as photos, blogs, tweets, FB posts, associated with specific locations, are very likely to know something about their locations that could potentially be useful for the user planning a road trip to or through these locations.

Solution Concept: Tag people who have uploaded location specific content as experts on that location. (This feature could be enhanced by rating the user's degree of expertise based on the volume and quality of uploaded content.) Target the road trip planner's queries to people in the network who are tagged as experts for the given location.

Kumar then started writing a design document that detailed out the implementation of this concept. His design document talked about adding a semantic tagging feature to the posts to capture location information and a design for analyzing the GPS[2] code of Flickr and Instagram pictures, travelogue reviews with more weightage to users based on the GPS location of their activity. This additional feature matched the locations mentioned in the query with relevant users and content.

Once the design document was done he thought he would try and get some sleep. However, he just couldn't stop his mind from racing ahead into the technical details of the semantic tagging feature.

He continued working non-stop all night, stopping only to wolf down a sandwich when day broke. He had some test data in his laptop. He wrote some scripts

---

2   GPS – Global Positioning System https://en.wikipedia.org/wiki/Global_Positioning_System

that simulated his semantic tagging logic. When he finally ran the scripts, the result was stupendous! His semantic tagging feature could identify specific locations in the posts 78% of the time.

Now all he had to do was use the identified location from the initial query to find users who were associated with the identified location. He was sure that by targeting the query to these select set of users, it would result in conversations which engage the user who was planning the road trip.

Kumar pumped his fist in the air. He had done it. He was now an innovator.

Fun Exercise:

Come up with a plausible hypothesis for the following complaint received from a customer of the Pontiac division of General Motors -

"This is the second time that I have written to you, and I don't blame you for not answering me, because I sounded crazy, but it is a fact that we have a tradition in our family of ice-cream for dessert after dinner each night, but the kind of ice-cream varies so, every night, after we've eaten, the whole family votes on which kind of ice-cream we should have and I drive down to the store to get it. It's also a fact that I recently purchased a new Pontiac and since then my trips to the store have created a problem....

You see, every time I buy vanilla ice cream, when I start back from the store my car won't start. If I get any other kind of ice cream, the car starts just fine. I want you to know I'm serious about this question, no matter how silly it sounds...

"What is it about a Pontiac that makes it not start when I get vanilla ice-cream, and easy to start whenever I get any other kind of ice-cream?"

Chapter 4
Knowing What You Don't Know

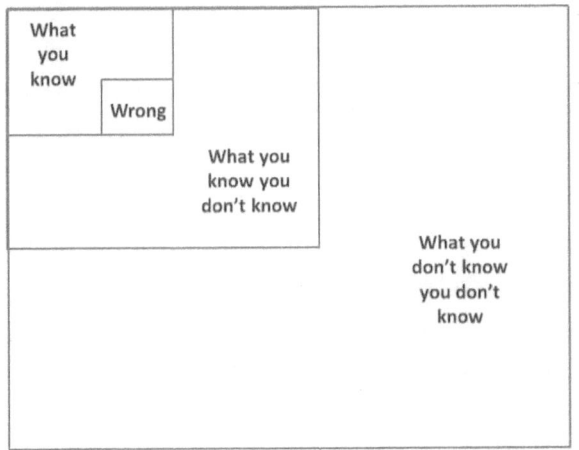

-Skip Walter

"Good start. You have your work cut out for you, Kumar," said Judith.

"Good start?" 'Good start' is what Kumar tells his nephews when they manage to fall only once from their bicycles. Nice people say 'good start' to cloak bad feedback. After all, ideas are like babies. People reserve the right to be jingoistic about theirs and everyone else gingerly walk on eggshells every time they are asked for an opinion. He remembered the bell curve model 'How Americans share feedback' posted by Octavian Costache on his blog[3].

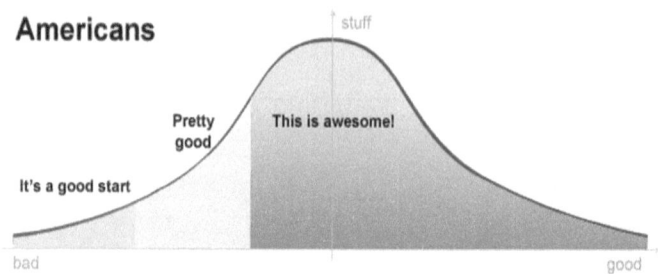

Kumar was chanting 'This is off the charts awesome' up until that moment. Judith's nonchalant reaction had burst his bubble.

Kumar felt the sheer weight of the sleepless night knocking him off the ground. He couldn't fathom why Judith didn't appreciate the ingenuity of his solution.

"I am sorry, I don't understand. What do you mean by 'Good start'? You make it sound like my solution is somehow incomplete. What more do I have to do? The way I see it, I have solved the problem already. This is going to be a breakthrough for my company" Kumar stood there, fumbling for words.

As soon as the flight landed at their layover point, he had rushed to find Judith to tell her how her advice had helped him. Her response felt anti-climactic.

---

3 https://medium.com/octavians-thoughts/what-does-its-a-good-start-really-mean-ff8c1a2495c4#.u3vq75qct

Judith didn't want to break his confidence either. But she knew that it's important to remind him that he is in a marathon and not a 100-meter dash.

"Kumar, I agree with you that this has the potential to move the needle. No doubt about that. I am impressed with your abductive thinking. You have applied the first discipline well. But, you haven't solved the problem yet. Let's get some coffee and discuss the second discipline."

Kumar followed Judith to the Cafe in silence, using every ounce of his energy to mask the disappointment that was tearing him apart. Judith waited for Kumar to finish his Espresso. And, then she took out her notepad and wrote down the second discipline.

"Kumar, the first discipline 'Embracing Ambiguity' helped you to discover a plausible hypothesis. You are ready for the next step 'Stitching the Big Picture'. The second discipline will help you to understand all the variables in the equation to align this hypothesis with your goal.

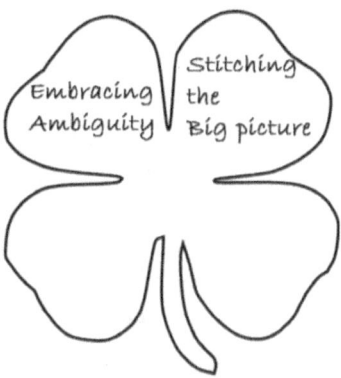

"Let me tell you about Thomas Alva Edison's legacy which demonstrates the merits of 'Stitching the Big Picture'. Edison was not the first person to come up with idea of the light bulb. But he believed that the value of an idea lies in the *'using'* of it. He accomplished that by stitching the big picture."

Kumar couldn't tell if it was the walk, the caffeine or a positive reaction to Judith bringing up Edison in the discussion. Something took the edge off his frustration. He understood that Judith meant what she said. She considered his solution a good start that needed some more work and she was willing to help him get there. It wasn't a polite way of telling him that his idea was bad. He took a deep breath and smiled.

"My friends and I used to have intense discussions on Edison during college days. I would love to understand how Edison's legacy is a testament to 'stitching the big picture? This sounds interesting!"

Judith was happy with Kumar's response. She continued with her explanation, "Edison was not just an inventor. Once he invented a new product he put in a lot of effort into designing and shaping the ecosystem that enabled his product to achieve a larger purpose. *Stitching the big picture* can mean understanding the ecosystem to leverage it to one's advantage. That has its own merits. However, for Edison it was also about controlling and shaping the ecosystem to fulfil his vision for the product. How would you define an ecosystem, Kumar?"

"Well, an ecosystem consists of different players coexisting in a shared system. If any one factor is changed or removed, it affects the balance of the entire ecosystem. So, one would need to consider all known and unknown partners and understand what any change would mean to the entire system. Is that what you mean by 'stitching the big picture'?" Kumar replied.

Judith was happy with how quickly Kumar was grasping things. "Kumar, you got it right. I find Edison a great role model for entrepreneurs. He transformed inventions to innovation with *a greater vision* of how his invention impacts the entire ecosystem. Let us try to understand this by looking at Edison's work with the light bulb.

Remember, this was a time when streets were lit up with gas or oil lamps and homes mostly had candle light. Edison's vision was to revolutionize the lighting business with electric powered light bulbs. In fact, he is known to have said, *'We will make electricity so cheap that only the rich will burn candles'*. He saw the invention of the light bulb as just one of the steps in pursuit of this greater vision."

"Are you with me so far?," Judith asked. Kumar nodded his head vigorously. Judith continued," Edison identified several problems he had to address to bring his greater vision to life. First, he had to of course make the light bulb robust, reliable and easy to manufacture to ensure that it was convenient and affordable to use in everyday life. Then he had to figure out how to build a power station that would power all the light bulbs. Edison planned how his invention could fit as part of the whole electrical system, including the power distribution, switches, meters and a new craft of lighting design. His industrial research lab combined electrical and chemical laboratories, as well as a machine shop. His team started developing electrical lighting components by 1880 in a new factory.

The first generating station was opened in September 1882 on Pearl Street in lower Manhattan. He also had to figure out the distribution of electricity from the generating station to the location of the lighting system. On January 19, 1883, the first standardized incandescent electric lighting system employing overhead wires began service in Roselle, New Jersey. Edison forged an enormous ecosystem consisting of power generation, distribution and electric lighting which eventually went on to replace the gas and oil based lighting utilities and eliminated candles as the primary source of lighting at homes."

"So Kumar, is this helpful? Do you now understand why I think you have more work to do before you can claim victory?" She could see that Kumar had gotten over his disappointment. He was deep in thought trying to figure out how to stitch together his own big picture.

After a few moments, she continued, "You have come up with an interesting idea that could significantly enhance your product. You now need to analyse how this idea impacts elements of the ecosystem around your product. You may even need to reshape or add elements to the ecosystem to make your idea successful."

Kumar replied, "I get that. But where do I start?"

Judith knew how to get him started. She said, "Let's try to follow the steps of Edison. He had a greater vision for his light bulb. What is the larger purpose for your app? If there is a singular truth that can guide all your stakeholders - users, employees, and influencers of the app, what would that be?"

The question stumped him like the sort of esoteric questions that have always confused him. His role was to build the product. He had also read the mission and vision statement of the company but couldn't remember it now. He thought hard but drew a blank.

"Why don't you try the app like a normal user, Kumar? Take your own time. See if you can articulate for yourself what purpose the app serves."

Kumar logged in to the app to plan a mock road trip, putting himself in the shoes of a user. After a few trials and some convoluted wordsmithing, he finally got it. And, when he did, he was surprised at the simplicity of the answer.

"Road Trip Genie gives people all the information and services they need to plan and manage amazing trips," he proclaimed.

Judith nodded, "Perfect. The app's value to the user is straightforward. They use the Road Trip Genie app to plan and manage their trips. If the app stays true its purpose, users will be happy. Now, take a step back to stitch the big picture. What are all the elements of the ecosystem that make your app successful at achieving its purpose?"

"Well, there are the content providers from whom we receive a lot of content for our users to browse and search through. Then there are the service providers who provide various travel related services," replied Kumar thoughtfully.

Judith prompted Kumar to continue, "Hasn't your new idea added new elements to the ecosystem? Don't these new elements influence the outcome for your users?"

Kumar replied without missing a beat "The experts are integral to the solution. They are the influencers. The tagging feature will be useless if they don't contribute."

Judith kept going, "Kumar, I am sure your company has put a lot of thought into how to engage content and service providers into the ecosystem. They would have designed incentive models for these partners to profitably participate in the business of serving your users. Now that you have introduced a new element, 'the experts', to your business model, you need to similarly figure out how you are going to drive their engagement in your ecosystem. The experts can help. Does that mean that they are *willing* to help too? Your partners should be both able and willing"

He hadn't thought through that. "How can I get them there? How do I motivate the experts to help the users?"

Fun Exercise:

Can you guess which management author used a variant of the following story in one of his many books on management?

One day a traveller, walking along a lane, came across 3 stonecutters working in a quarry. Each was busy cutting a block of stone. Interested to find out what they were working on, he asked the first stonecutter what he was doing. "I am cutting a stone!" Still no wiser the traveller turned to the second stonecutter and asked him what he was doing. "I am cutting this block of stone to make sure that it's square, and its dimensions are uniform, so that it will fit exactly in its place in a wall." A bit closer to finding out what the stonecutters were working on but still unclear, the traveller turned to the third stonecutter. He seemed to be the happiest of the three and when asked what he was doing, replied: **"I am building a cathedral."**

Chapter 5
Facing Facts

I have steadily endeavoured to keep my mind free so as to give up any hypothesis, however much beloved (and I cannot resist forming one on every subject), as soon as the facts are shown to be opposed to it.

-Charles Darwin

When Kumar finally settled into his seat for the final stretch of the journey to San Francisco, he was exhausted. He had worked on his idea all through the first leg of the journey. And, the sleep debt came back to collect. He dozed off as soon as the plane hit cruising altitude. However, he did not sleep for long. He never could sleep much when he had unfinished business.

Judith had left him with a question before they boarded the flight. "The experts are *able* to help. Does that mean that they are *willing* to help too? Your partners should be both able and willing"

Now Kumar understood what Judith meant when she said that he had his work cut out for him. His idea was just the invention. He now had to figure out how to get his invention to fit into the larger ecosystem of his product and its business of delivering the best road trip experience possible for their users. For this to work he had to figure out how to motivate the experts to engage in the process of helping users.

"How can I get them there? How do I motivate the experts to help the users?"

Now that he understood what he needed to do, his mind started churning again. He had recently read about how using gaming principles enhanced engagement of users and motivated them to contribute more and associate more deeply with the ecosystem. He decided to develop a gamification model that would drive engagement of experts in Road Trip Genie.

As he started building this model, he realized that the experts are the actual genies in Road Trip Genie. Their social reputation and influence in the ecosystem would grow based on their expertise and engagement in the app.

He wondered how the company leadership would take to this new idea. What he was proposing brought a whole new dimension to the term "genie" in Road Trip Genie. The app would serve as the lamp that hosts these genies.

He had to develop the gamification model to incentivize experts for their participation in Road Trip Genie. He started working on a reputation algorithm to rate experts based on a combination of their contributions to the app and feedback from the users.

He also came up with an incentive program for rewarding the experts with free products and services from the service provider partners in the app.

For a moment, Kumar felt that his plan was a slam dunk. But then he soon realized the massive amount of work this entailed only when he turned his attention to the implementation roadmap. There was a lot of user interface functionality that would have to be developed to manage profiles of these experts in the app. He had to build safeguards in the model to ensure that experts could not game the system to earn undeserved rewards. As he continued documenting the design details, his notes ran into scores of pages.

He then started outlining a project plan for implementing the gamification capability in Road Trip Genie. His most optimistic plan required 5 months. He just couldn't see a way of getting this done sooner. He knew this just wouldn't fly. His CTO certainly would not want to wait for 5 months to see if his new idea could save Road Trip Genie. His mood turned despondent again.

The crew announced their arrival at San Francisco. Kumar was eager to find Judith at the baggage claim area. He had developed a lot of confidence in her. If there was anyone who could help him, it was her.

As soon as Judith saw Kumar rushing towards her at the baggage claim area, she knew what was wrong. She asked him, "So, you have created your project plan haven't you?"

Kumar was puzzled. How could she know? She was seated in business class and couldn't have seen him filling in all those spreadsheets huddled in his economy class seat. He cast his confusion aside and jumped straight to the point. "It is going to take me at least 5 months to develop this. That's not quick enough! What do I do now?"

Judith calmly responded, "Hold your horses, young man! Can you list out for me all the work you will be doing in the 5 months?"

Kumar had all this neatly planned in his head. He did not need to refer to his notes. He provided Judith a quick summary, "In the first two sprints we will build the features that enable the app to identify experts based on the content they have produced - photos, tweets, blogs, etc. and to connect the user queries to the most appropriate experts. Then we need four sprints for the gamification model. There is a lot of work here, both on the UI side and the algorithms in the back end. These six sprints will consume three months. After this we need at least two months for system integration, testing, code hardening, etc."

Judith smiled patiently, "Ok, now tell me what is the real problem here. Is it that it's going to take you a long time to develop the solution or that you are not sure that the solution will save Road Trip Genie?"

Kumar sighed, "You are right, the bigger question is whether this innovation will solve the user dropout problem. I wish there is a way to find this out before we build this whole solution. I don't think we can wait for five months to find out if this solution will work. And if it doesn't, then we would have wasted five months of engineering effort as well."

Judith waved an imaginary magic wand and said, "Your wish is granted. There is a way to tease out the risks and improve the chances of success of your innovative solution. You will need to abandon the project plan you have created. Follow the hypothesis testing approach instead."

"What's that?," Kumar asked impatiently.

"Well, my bags are here and my ride is waiting outside. Let me give you a few pointers and leave you to research this on your own."

Judith quickly scribbled the third discipline on her notepad

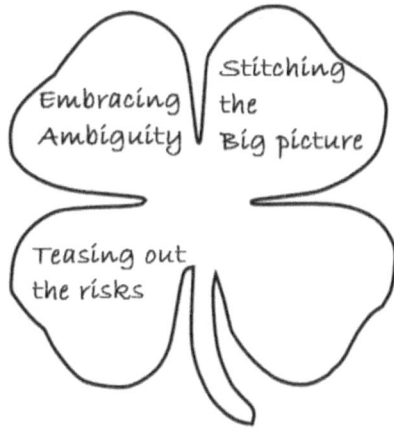

"Remember that when you practiced the first and second disciplines of innovation you developed

a number of hypotheses. Your innovation is based on these hypotheses. Before you go and build your solution, you need to test each of your hypothesis. The results from your tests will tell if you are right. And if you are not you can refine your hypothesis and tweak the solution. Pick the hypothesis that poses the biggest risk to your product's success first and then progressively work through them one by one. If you design your experiments in a way where you are incrementally building features as part of your hypothesis testing approach, your confidence in the solution will grow with each iteration. Another way of looking at it is that you are teasing out the risks in your solution with each iteration starting with the worst risks first."

"Wow, that's a lot to grasp in 30 seconds. Where can I learn more?" Kumar was getting anxious. He was worried about whether he would be able to figure this out by himself.

"Search the web for how Nordstrom's Innovation lab operates. And here is my Business Card and the notepad that we used to discuss the disciplines. Let's meet for lunch next weekend. Email me." said Judith and walked out of the terminal building.

Kumar had seen the Nordstrom store at the mall on his last visit to the US. He did not know anything about them other than that they were a retail chain in the US. His curiosity was aroused. What could Nordstrom's innovation lab teach him? What was so special about how they operated? He couldn't wait to get to his hotel room to start his research.

Fun Exercise:

In the following chart one line (the blue one) represents the number of motor vehicles in the US. Can you guess what the other line represents? What event do you think caused the inflection point of these lines in the year 1913?

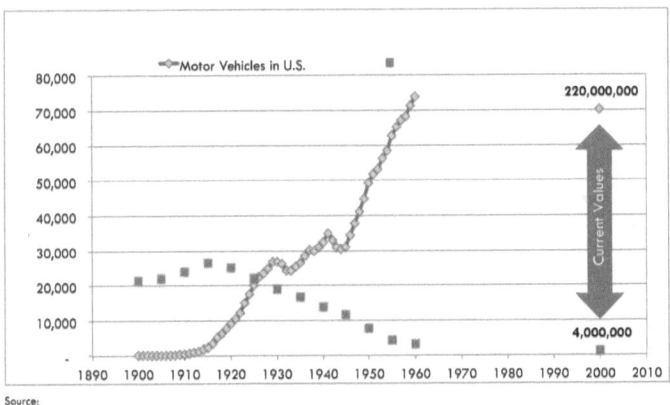

Chapter 6
Failing Fast

Failure is an option here. If you are not failing, you are not innovating enough

-*Elon Musk*

Kumar sensed a different world when he stepped out of the SFO terminal to hail a cab. A stranger smiled and waved at him "GOOD DAY!! How do you do?" He waved back and smiled. A good day indeed!

He stifled a chuckle when he spotted a bright red cab named 'Big Dog City'. 'Nothing else would do' he told himself when he got into that cab. The cheerful driver lived up to the funky name. Kumar's first ride in SFO started with a bang!

He reached his hotel room in 30 minutes. His room had a good view of the Golden Gate bridge and he had one more day before his meeting with the board. As tempting as that was, Kumar decided that touring could wait and started googling instead to learn more about Nordstrom. All the articles about Nordstrom that Kumar found on the internet made very complimentary statements about the company -

'Nordstrom is a high-end fashion retailer, in business for over a century . . . . ranked around #250 in the Fortune 500 list . . . outperforming other retail companies consistently . . . They set the high bar for customer service in the retail industry.'

But the thing that caught Kumar's attention specifically was something that he found in a Forbes article dated August 14th, 2015. It said, '. . . Nordstrom is doing all the right things to address the way today's consumer likes to shop. For example, the company is doing a lot to serve the customer who shops using a mobile device. . . . Nordstrom is also developing new exciting new concepts that appeal to millennials. . . . their strategies and merchandising are what drive consumers to buy, not price promotions. . . . Next year the plan is to reduce sale events by an additional 25%.'

Kumar knew that fashion retailing is a very competitive business. Fashion trends are very volatile and retailers had to be agile to win in this game. When retailers' fashion predictions didn't play out in the market, they would end up having to hold discount sales. How was Nordstrom winning this game? How were they able to feel the pulse of the shopper better than anyone else? More importantly, how were they able to do it repeatedly and consistently in the fast-changing fashion world? They must have figured out a technique to tease out the risks? That must certainly be why Judith wanted him to study them.

Kumar continued looking for content about Nordstrom on the internet. That's when he chanced upon the blog of Eric Ries, the creator of the Lean Startup methodology. One of Eric's blogs was about Nordstrom's innovation lab[4]. Embedded in the blog was a video clip of a Nordstrom team building an app that helps shoppers choose sunglasses. The process of building the app was simply amazing. Kumar couldn't even imagine that software could be developed this way. The video clip starts with a shot of Nordstrom's app development team walking into a Nordstrom store and occupying a table on the store floor. They start by pulling some of the store associates into a brainstorming exercise without any preconceived set of requirements. They walk through the steps of how a shopper selects a set of sunglasses and then come up with some hypotheses of what might help the shopper. They test their hypotheses by developing corresponding features for their app. The software development work is done on the store floor. As they develop each feature, they load it on to an iPad and hand it over to the sales associates who then offer it to shoppers to try out. Feedback is immediately incorporated into the next iteration of software development. The whole process from start to finish takes just one week. At the end of the week they have an app that the shoppers absolutely love!

Eric's blog talks about how Nordstrom has taken the *'get out of the building'* concept in Toyota's

---

4 http://www.startuplessonslearned.com/2011/10/case-study-nordstrom-innovation-lab.html

production system to a whole different level. They actually conduct the entire process of detailing out requirements, developing the code, testing it, gathering feedback and iterating over, all in the store. The idea evolves from a hypothesis to a concrete product over multiple rapid iterations. Each iteration teases out risks that are identified by observing actual usage of the feature by sales associates and shoppers. Risks that otherwise could have led to the shopper abandoning the app can now be addressed immediately. This was an eye opener for Kumar. He had always been an enthusiastic practitioner of Agile methodology. However, his projects had always involved product managers building a backlog of requirements and his team working off the pool of requirements in Agile style iterations. Product managers gave feedback after each iteration. However, customer feedback was gathered only after beta launch. No wonder so many innovative products fail when the rubber meets the road.

After this, Kumar found other examples of Nordstrom's unique application development process. There was another texting app that they had built which let shoppers exchange messages with in-store sales associates for help with buying shoes, clothes and other products. This app had started life as an email based app but then was quickly moved over to a texting platform based on customer response during the development cycle. A number of features in this app were a result of the dynamic participation of customers and sales associates directly in the development process. Nordstrom's process truly mitigated major risks in developing new innovations. All innovations came with major risks. After all they are based on some hypothesis and not on an established principle that is guaranteed to work. Nordstrom's process allowed them to test the hypothesis rapidly. If the hypothesis is validated, they proceed and incrementally build the next feature. If not, then they have failed fast and therefore can quickly pivot the idea and start over with minimal delay and wastage of resources.

Kumar knew what he had to do. He started noting down all the hypothesis underlying his innovation -

1. We can identify experts with knowledge about road trip destinations by the GPS tags of content they have uploaded such as photos, blogs, tweets, FB posts
2. Experts will be motivated to respond to user queries if they can compete for social reputation within the app (Gamification)
3. Service providers will sponsor rewards for experts because they will see value in their active participation in the app
4. Responses from experts will be very helpful for users as they plan their road trips and hence they will not drop out of the app

He now had to design experiments to test each of these hypotheses.

He tore up the project plan that he had prepared earlier. In its place, he created four mini-plans - one for each of the hypothesis that he had listed out. Each mini-plan detailed out four activities - (i) tasks involved in building a prototype of the features required to test the hypothesis; (ii) a plan for testing the hypothesis with actual users; (iii) refining the prototype based on feedback from the testing; (iv) integration of the features into the main codebase

He then mapped the four mini-plans to a time-line. His timeline showed that he could have a prototype of the features related to identifying experts and directing queries to them in a matter of days. After that his plan was to engage actual expert users and develop gamification features using Nordstrom's approach of active participation of users in the process. Allowing for two months of iterative feature development, he would have a *'customer-tested and proven'* gamification model in less than half the time taken in his previous plan. If the gamification approach did not work, then he would have to pivot. On the other hand, if it worked, the rest of the project would be a breeze.

As he reviewed the revised plan, he realized the value of the hypothesis-testing approach. He had identified all the risks in his innovation by listing all the hypotheses that his innovation was based on. Then he had prioritized the risks in terms of their potential for derailing the project and created mini-plans to validate the riskiest ones first. This way, once the critical risks were mitigated, the project was well on its way to success. If any of the critical risks turned out to be show-stoppers, he could go back to the drawing board early in the project rather than finding out too late that the project was going to fail.

He felt a lot more confident of presenting this approach to the CTO. He had heard his CTO use the term *'fail-fast'* before. It made more sense to him now than when he had first heard the term.

Fun Exercise:

#1 in circulation on day 1 of launch! Can you guess which media company achieved this position in almost every city that it launched its daily newspaper in?

Chapter 7
Kintsukuroi

Kintsukuroi "to repair with gold" is the Japanese art of repairing broken pottery with lacquer dusted or mixed with powdered gold, silver, or platinum. The repaired product becomes a cherished work of art.

Kumar passed through a colourful workspace with a splattering of coffee machines and ping pong tables to reach the boardroom. The monotone industrial decor of the board room was a stark contrast to the vibrant workspaces around.

The founders Meredith Scully and Rahul Patel looked uncomfortable, flanked by the board members. After a quick round of introductions, Kumar began to set up his presentation. He mentally assigned each of the board members a different identity, a trick he learned in a public speaking class. So here in the intimidating board room, he spotted a few of his favourite characters from movies.

1. Board member 1 was Tony Stark from Iron Man. Flamboyant and charming, he had the look of someone who doesn't suffer fools gladly.

2. Board member 2, the elderly gentleman was Tywin Lannister from Game of thrones. Astute and pragmatic, he didn't need words for anyone to understand that he was in charge.

3. Board member 3, was Mogambo from Mr. India because when he said "Happy to meet you" while shaking hands, that sounded like "Mogambo khush hua"

Tony Stark pursed his lips and sighed. Kumar could tell that he had already written off Road Trip Genie in his mind and considered this meeting a waste of time. "Ok, Kumar. Give us a run-down of the new plan. Go!"

Kumar had prepared a detailed slide deck for the meeting but the board seemed to be in a hurry. He closed his laptop, scanned the room once more and started.

"Who is the Genie?," Kumar asked his audience. On Kumar's first day at the company, the CTO had spent a lot of time talking about the vision for their product. At that time, Kumar was sold on the idea that their app would deliver a "genie-like" wow experience to their users.

"The app, of course. Well, I hope it remains so. We have invested enough on this ludicrous Genie" Mogambo chuckled.

Kumar smiled nervously. He wasn't sure how the board would react to what he was going to say next. "Our app is designed to serve a large number of users with diverse profiles and interests. Don't you think our users will be better served if we had many genies with varied expertise to cater to diverse interests? And how about if our genies were humans who could relate to and empathize with users better than a software app could?"

The board members were starting to look confused. Kumar had to clarify quickly. Else his audience would tune out soon. "Let me get straight to the point," he said. "I am proposing a modification to our product strategy. The social features in our app will be redesigned to identify experts in our user base. These experts will help other users in planning and managing their road trips. Matching of experts to user requests will be done based on the destinations that experts have knowledge of. Thus, our experts are the genies because they help our users in making the right choices - akin to granting wishes."

Tony Stark rolled his eyes "Please don't start singing 'Genie in a Bottle' now. Our app is the bottle. Is that it?"

Kumar looked around at the others. He was relieved to see that he had not lost them. They were not being dismissive. However, there was a questioning look in their eyes. He was sure they had a lot of questions. He wanted to make his case before the volley of questions hit him. He continued, "A fine bottle to boot. Our app is doing a good job of collecting and curating destination content. Our users have raved about the quality of content that our app serves up. They also like the fact that they can reach out to others to seek help. However, this is where we lost the plot. The help that they receive from their social network is either inadequate or inappropriate. That is why they mostly disengage from the app after initiating a query. My hypothesis is that if the queries were directed at experts, people who have some knowledge of the destination of interest, then our users would find more value in the conversation. My recommendation is to do away with the current social feature that lets people ask questions to their immediate connections. Instead, we nurture users with knowledge about destinations, our genies. Crowdsourcing has proven to be successful in many other areas. I am confident this can be made to work for us too."

"Hold your horses, young man," interjected Meredith. "You are proposing a radical change to the product. Before we race down this path, I would like to know if all options with the current approach have been explored. Why don't we expand the reach of the query to more of the users' connections, maybe second and third degree connections?"

Kumar was ready for that question. "We thought of that. In fact, we tried it out. Our simulation showed that the number of first respondents increased to about double the current number. However, the number of continued conversations that result out of the first responses is still very small. The quality of the engagement does not improve. The likelihood that a respondent has detailed knowledge about the destination does not improve materially. Hence, it is very likely that users will still disengage in large numbers since they don't get the value they seek from these conversations. Additionally, larger number of responses from distant connections will likely result in a higher percentage of spam. This could deteriorate user experience in our app. Our user engagement problem is better solved by people who have knowledge about destinations and road trip routes."

"How would you accurately identify such people" Mogambo asked, resting his head on his hand.

Kumar could sense that his idea was drawing them in. "People who have uploaded content such as blogs, pictures, tweets, Facebook posts etc. associated with specific locations are most likely to know something about their locations. Adding a GPS tagging feature to the posts will capture location information. Analyzing the GPS of Flickr and Instagram pictures, travelogue reviews and GPS tags of users' content will help us identify the destination experts. We have run some estimates using my GPS tagging script and found that we can identify locations of 78% of user content. I know we can improve this with enhancements to our user interfaces to enable capture of GPS locations at the time users post their content."

"That sounds good. But how will you get these experts to join your band. The previous version was supposed to work because people trust their friends. Now, these experts are strangers. Why should they help?" Tony Stark asked without any trace of sarcasm. Kumar counted that as a win. And luckily, Kumar was prepared for this question too. "Think gamification. I am building a reputation algorithm to rate the experts based on a combination of their contributions to the app and feedback from the users. We can also develop an incentive program for rewarding the experts with free products and services from the service provider partners in the app."

"Crowdsourcing! Gamification! … Give us a timeline, Kumar. Let's face the facts. This unicorn is dying. Will you save it on time?" Tywin Lannistor spoke for the first time.

Kumar was thankful for the structured approach that Judith had taught him. His idea had taken seed. The board was not shooting his proposal down outright. They just need him to execute fast and the third leaf in Judith's clover had shown him the way to achieve that. He replied to Tywin, "My approach is to tease out the risks one by one with phased iterations by involving a beta testing group. The prototype of the features related to identifying experts and directing queries to them will be completed in a week. This will be our Minimum Viable Product (MVP). After that, we will engage the actual expert users and develop the gamification features by studying their active participation. The algorithms will also be tweaked in phases. This process will take another two months. We will have a customer-tested and validated gamification model in less than two and a half months. We will be building this product with the experts and users in the trenches. The product will evolve as per the needs of the users and experts. They will own the success of this product because it will be their product too."

The board found his plan intriguing and extended the session by another hour to discuss the implementation plan that he had prepared.

Kumar was feeling very confident now. He thought that the battle was won. Things had gone much better than he had expected, . . . until Tywin Lannistor spoke up again. "Kumar, I am sure that my colleagues will agree when I say that you have come up with a really innovative solution. No doubt about that. Frankly, we were ready to pull the plug on this product today. Now we believe that you have a workable turnaround plan. However, for us to back this plan we need to see visible progress weekly. The only measure of progress that I will accept is number of experts that you are able to convert into genies . . ."

Kumar quickly replied, "I don't see a problem with that. I am confident that our algorithm for mining our content to identify experts will work. I will send you weekly reports . . ."

Tywin impatiently interrupted him, "You did not let me finish. Your algorithm may be good. However, remember that most of our users look for remote, off-the-beaten-path kind of destinations. The marketing team's last report shows a list of destinations stack ranked by popularity in our user base. We couldn't collectively recognize about half the destinations in the top 100 names on that list. Do you think that you will find experts for all these destinations within our user base? I think not. You will have to reach outside of our current user base to find some of your genies. So, the measure that I would like you to report on is the number of genies by destination, stack ranked by popularity of destinations."

Tywin had lived up to the reputation of his character in Game of Thrones. He had delivered a thunderbolt that completely shattered Kumar's confidence. Tywin was right. Most people had hardly even heard of many of the popular road trip destinations in their app. How was he going to find his genies?

Surprisingly, it was Tony Stark who came to his aid. "Friends, this is a risk worth taking. Our appetite for risks got us here. Kumar's approach completely overhauls how this company has approached product development. He is reinventing the app along with the product development process. I am very curious to see how this all turns out. I propose that we give him a chance."

Tony turned around to face Kumar and continued, "Kumar, your innovative approach to this problem is brilliant. We also like the lean and agile implementation plan that incrementally teases out risks along the way. We grant you the 3 months that you seek to implement your plan. Additionally, here's what you need to do. Figure out how you are going to attract experts from outside our user base. Our marketing team is already researching destinations on our top 100 list. They can put you on the relevant forums both online and offline if that helps. Remember that we will be closely tracking your progress on growing the number of genies across our long list of popular destinations."

Tony then called for a vote on this proposal.

Meredith Scully and Rahul Patel sighed in relief when everyone voted in favour of the plan. They had entered that board room fearing that the board members had already made up their minds and the meeting would end up a farce. But Kumar had saved the day. Now would he be able to save their unicorn? He had a solid plan. Would he be able to build a cohort of genies that had knowledge of destinations far and wide?

Fun Exercise:

Fill in the empty box in the picture below.

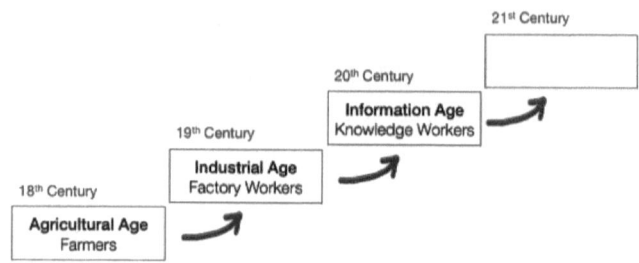

Chapter 8
Vortex

Just as ripples spread out when a single pebble is dropped into water, the actions of individuals can have far-reaching effects.

-Dalai Lama

Kumar was swept up by an avalanche of emotions when he walked out of that board room. He had just promised them a legion of Genies. Was he getting ahead of himself? His head hurt.

BEEP!

That was a message from Judith inviting him for dinner after office hours. Kumar sighed in relief and quickly confirmed back. He had got this far with her guidance. Perhaps, she would help him hit a homerun with this one.

As soon as Kumar stepped into the restaurant, he realised that it was like nothing he had ever seen before. He wasn't prepared for what he saw in there. 'Is this really a restaurant?', he thought, all the while scanning the happy faces around him. The day's special menu displayed outside only piqued his curiosity. A nice lady guided him to the table where Judith was seated. If it weren't for her uniform T-shirt, he wouldn't have been able to tell whether she was one of the staff or a friend of Judith who just happened to be there.

"Lovely to see you again, Kumar. Hope you had a great meeting today."

"Thanks for inviting me, Judith. I am so happy to see you again! What kind of restaurant is this? The menu card says that the food is free. But, how?"

Judith smiled "I can see why this is confusing. This restaurant is part of a chain called Karma Kitchen[5]. There is no price for food. But that doesn't mean that it ought to be free. Our meal is free but we can choose to pay for people who visit the restaurant after us. And, we also choose how much."

The engineer in Kumar was intrigued "I don't understand. How does this business work?"

Judith continued with a smile "The staff that you see here are all volunteers. The volunteers believe in the gift economy and offer the meals to the guests as a genuine gift. Guests make contributions to complete the cycle and pay it forward for the guests who come after them. Karma Kitchen doesn't need marketing because their customers do that for them with viral videos, Instagrams, and blogs. Their tagline 'Growing in Generosity' resonates well with their phenomenal growth from a single restaurant in Berkeley on March 31st, 2007 to a global chain of restaurants"

---

5   http://www.karmakitchen.org/story.php

"Wow! What a concept!" Kumar exclaimed. "I am sure you have a reason for picking this place for us to meet at."

Judith laughed, "You are right. I wanted to give you a memorable story to remember the fourth discipline. But more on that later. Why don't you tell me how your presentation to the board worked out?"

Kumar was eager to share his dilemma with Judith. He quickly recapped the proceedings from the board meeting for Judith. He dwelt at length on how Tywin had delivered a thunderbolt at the end. He explained to her how Road Trip Genie's users overwhelmingly preferred little known destinations and how Tywin had latched on to this little nugget of information. The success of his turnaround plan now depended on his ability to build a legion of genies who were experts on little known destinations. Tony Stark had offered him the marketing team's support. But it was his problem to solve. The board had made it clear that he was accountable for the results. Kumar just did not get this.

He asked Judith, "Why me? I am not the marketing guy. I am the innovator. I came up with the idea. I figured out how to stitch the big picture together. I even came up with the approach that will tease out the risks. I know I can build a wonderful product. Shouldn't the marketing guys figure out how to get people to use the product? Why is the board making this my problem? They were unanimous in their opinion that my idea is brilliant. If they truly believe that, they should let me focus on building the product and direct the marketing guys to build the legion of genies. I don't know the first thing about marketing. I am just an engineer."

Judith couldn't stop smiling. She knew many engineers like Kumar. Engineers who just shied away from marketing and wanted to have nothing to do with it. She empathized with Kumar. "I realize you have a lot to do in the next three months. However, I also agree with the board. You must take the lead in building the legion of genies. This whole innovation is your idea. You have a deep understanding of how all the different pieces come together. No one can speak about this with the level of conviction that you can. Don't shirk this responsibility."

Kumar let out a sigh, "You too, Judith? I thought you would take my side and come up with ideas on how I could push this responsibility to the marketing team. Anyway, please help me understand why you think I should take the lead on this."

Judith was prepared for this, "Kumar, this is where the fourth discipline comes in. A successful innovator needs to know how to earn social currency."

Kumar had come across the term 'social currency' in an article on web marketing but had not paid much attention to it. He said, "I am sure that this has something to do with marketing. I still don't get why an innovator should bother with it. I don't believe that innovations become successful because someone hypes them up."

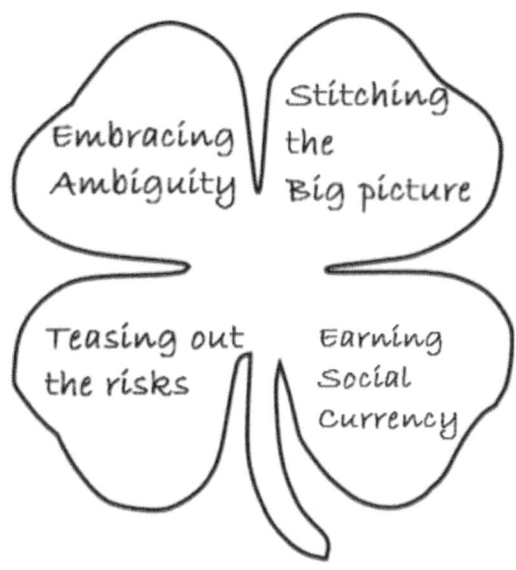

Judith patient as always, replied calmly, "Tell me, how do you keep yourself up-to-date on the latest available technologies? Say for example you wanted to evaluate the suitability of a new technology like Hadoop for a problem you are working on, who would you turn to?"

Without a second thought, Kumar replied, "That's easy. I am a regular visitor on all the top tech forums. There are many techies there who are always discussing the latest tech developments and helping each other. In fact, I know some of the guys who have written parts of the Hadoop software. They hang out on these forums."

Judith pressed on. "Would you trust the inputs that you got on these forums?"

Kumar promptly replied, "Of course, if it came from one of the experts on the forum or was vetted by them, there would be no reason to doubt its quality. These guys take pleasure in sharing knowledge. They truly believe that open discussions about their work improves the quality and impact of their work."

Judith persisted with her line of questioning, "What happens when someone brings up a new idea on these forums? Do they get a good reception? What happens if the idea runs contrary to a widely accepted viewpoint?"

Kumar had seen this happen often. He said, "It all depends. Flawed ideas and ideas that aren't well thought out get shot down quickly. On the other hand, if it is a powerful idea and the owner of the idea is able to present a strong case for it, it leads to a lot of excitement. There are of course naysayers and harsh critics always. But if the idea is good, people discuss and share the idea widely and the feedback from these discussions help improve it further. The owner of the idea of course earns a lot of respect, especially if it is a contrarian idea. Original thought counts for a lot on these forums if you can speak with conviction about it."

Judith had not expected that it was going to be this easy to explain the fourth discipline to Kumar. She said to him, "Kumar, you have a lot more experience in earning social currency than I do. All the interactions on these tech forums that you described are about folks like you earning social currency. You freely share your knowledge and ideas with others. The only expectation of reward that you have is that you will receive help when you seek it and that you will get authentic feedback that will help you improve upon your ideas. Your contributions on these forums grow your reputation which in turn earns you the attention of others on the forum. The more your contributions are valued, the more widely they get dispersed and you are able to garner more attention from your audience."

Kumar suddenly became quiet and thoughtful. "Ok, but what does this have to do with marketing and with building a legion of genies?"

Judith knew from Kumar's body language that he was hooked. He was trying to connect the dots. She just had to prod him along. She continued with her explanation, "Marketing is all about building awareness of your product and its value proposition. Old school marketing strategies involved the marketer reaching out directly to the target audience via advertising and publicity campaigns to build awareness. Marketing strategies are successful when the audience is paying attention. Over the years as more and more marketers attempt to reach out to audiences who have less and less time to spare, this kind of marketing has become increasingly ineffective. Attention from audiences is no longer easy to garner."

This was resonating with Kumar. He interrupted Judith, "You are absolutely right. I hardly pay any attention to the advertisements on TV and in the

Newspaper, these days. And the direct marketing email that I get in my inbox; they automatically get discarded by my spam filter. I wonder how anyone can get a message across to a target audience in this environment of poor attention."

"Well," Judith replied, "this is where earning social currency is important. People who have a lot of social currency garner a lot of attention. By the way that is true for businesses too. Of course, if you abuse the system by using the attention for blatant, over-the-top advertising your social currency goes down the drain. On the other hand, if you use the attention for sharing of your ideas and authentic messages, you earn a loyal fan following and even more social currency. Another advantage of this approach is that you don't need to directly touch every member of your target audience unlike the old-school marketing approach. If your idea or message is share-worthy, people will willingly share it with others and if all goes well you have it spreading like a virus on its own, without any additional push from you."

Kumar was engrossed in thought. He began to develop a sincere appreciation for the marketing function now. However, he still had an unanswered question. "Ok, I get that social currency is important for marketing in today's world but does it have to be done by me? Couldn't we assign a marketing person with the right skills to handle marketing of our product?"

"Oh, of course! I am sure you have some great people in your marketing team who are well versed with the concept of social currency. It is certainly their job to handle marketing for the product. But we are not talking about marketing of the product or building your company's brand. We are talking about building a legion of genies who will become part of your product's ecosystem. Who do you think has the credibility to earn social currency in the community of potential genies? You came up with this innovative idea. You can present it with conviction. You are introducing new concepts like gamification to a community of road trip enthusiasts for whom this may be a unique idea. Don't you think you as the originator of the idea will be able to drive more excitement and engagement by directly interacting with potential genies than a marketing person acting as your proxy? When we were talking about your tech forums, you mentioned the excitement that new ideas generate when the idea owners present them well. Now do you see why you should take the lead on this?"

Kumar was deep in thought. He could only nod his head in agreement.

Judith had more to say on this topic. So, she went on, "Sophisticated solutions like the one you are developing cannot be built in isolation. They need to be seamlessly integrated into the ecosystem in which they will function. Therefore, innovators like you need to become good at earning social currency. Social currency will buy you the support you will need from the ecosystem for your innovation to be successful. You have a brilliant idea for Road Trip Genie. It has the potential to become a highly successful product. Now go share your idea with the world and earn your social currency which will help you build the right ecosystem for it."

Kumar was sold on the idea of earning social currency. He was thinking ahead. "If my idea is truly unique and brilliant and I am able to present it with conviction in the right forums, people will pay attention. Then it is a question of whether they will share the idea with others."

"Yes, that's right," said Judith. "Now think about what motivates people to share. People are very likely to share things that are extra-ordinary, unique, new and impactful. Basically, something that creates an impression on the audience's mind. Anthropologists believe that this behaviour is driven by our desire to appear knowledgeable, well-informed or just cool."

Kumar interjected, "You know Judith, I was planning to write a post on Facebook about Karma Kitchen because the concept is so intriguing. I can already visualize a very passionate discussion with my friends on Facebook on this topic. I would never have thought about this as earning social currency."

Judith smiled with the realization that Kumar had mastered the four disciplines of Innovation. The confused young man at the airport had morphed into an innovator in the making. She had done her bit. Now it was up to Kumar to put his learning into practice.

Her parting comments to him were "Kumar, now go create your own story about your brilliant innovation. Find the right forums where you can share it. Present your innovative ideas in ways that people find easy to share with others. Involve them in developing and evolving the ideas. You know you will have succeeded when people start conversations with 'Hey, did you hear that Road Trip Genie is building a gamification feature.' or 'Hey, guess what! Nomadic Bill just signed up as a genie'. Before long, you would have created an epidemic with the legion of genies that you promised your Board. As a wise man once said '**Nothing is more powerful than an idea whose time has come**'."

Fun Exercise:

Earn your own social currency by participating in the following exercise.

Find a story, case study, factoid, or any other interesting titbit that either supports or debunks any of the ideas presented in this book and post it here - **www.theinnovationimperative.org**

We will enable voting buttons on all valid entries. We will also provide sharing options for you to share your post on your social networking channels. Get your friends to vote on your posts. Leader boards will be published on the website.

Appendix

Answers to Fun Exercises

Chapter 1:

It took 2000 litres of mold culture fluid to obtain enough pure Penicillin to treat single case of sepsis in a human. Scientists had to find a higher yielding variety of mold and then develop mutation and filtration techniques that ultimately produced 1000 times as much Penicillin as the first batches from Penicillium Notatum.

http://www.pbs.org/newshour/rundown/the-real-story-behind-the-worlds-first-antibiotic/

Chapter 2:

Scoring Key:

High scores indicate an intolerance of ambiguity. Having high intolerance means that you tend to perceive situations as threatening rather than promising. Lack of information or uncertainty would tend to make you uncomfortable. Ambiguity arises from three primary sources: novelty, complexity, and insolubility. These three subscales are measured by the instrument.

In scoring the instrument, the *even-numbered* items must be reversed. That is, 7 becomes 1, 6 becomes 2, 5 becomes 3, 3 becomes 5, 2 becomes 6, and 1 becomes 7. After reversing the appropriate items, sum all 16 items to get your score.

ITEM	SUBSCALE	ITEM	SUBSCALE	ITEM	SUBSCALE	ITEM	SUBSCALE
1	I	5	C	9	N	13	N
2	N	6	C	10	C	14	C
3	I	7	C	11	N	15	C
4	C	8	C	12	I	16	C

N = Novelty Score (2, 9, 11, 13) _____
C = Complexity Score (4, 5, 6, 7, 8, 10, 14, 16) _____
I = Insolubility Score (1, 3, 12) _____
Total Score _____

Chapter 3:

It took the customer less time to buy vanilla ice cream than other flavours because being the most popular flavour, it was stored near the front of the store. The others were at the back and it took considerably longer to check out the flavour. The extra time taken to get the other flavours allowed the engine to cool down sufficiently to start straight away. When vanilla was bought the engine did not have sufficient time to cool down causing a problem called as 'vapour lock'.

Chapter 4:

Peter Drucker used a variant of this story in his book, The Practice of Management. In Peter Drucker's version, when asked what they were doing, the first stonecutter replied: "I am making a living." The second kept on hammering while he said: "I am doing the best job of stone cutting in the entire Country." The third stonecutter, when asked the same question said: **"I am building a cathedral."**

Chapter 5:

The other line represents the number of Horses and Mules in the US. In 1913, Henry Ford installed the first moving assembly line for the Model T. It reduced the time to build a car from more than 12 hours to one and a half.

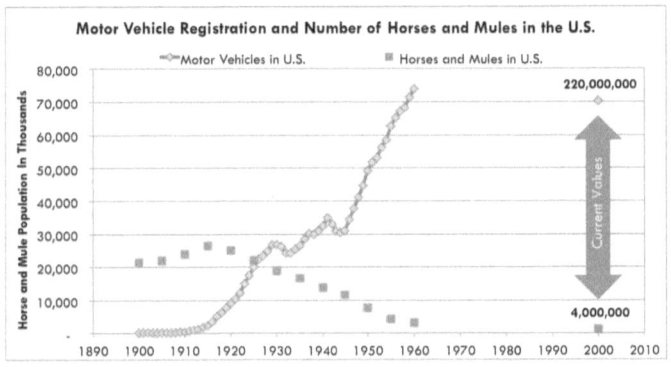

Chapter 6:

Dainik Bhaskar. In Jaipur, its first city of launch outside Madhya Pradesh, Dainik Bhaskar entered the market as number one with 172,000 copies on 19th December 1996. In its next new market, Chandigarh, it was again number one with 69,000 copies when it launched in May 2000. In its third launch - the state of Haryana - it entered as number one with 271,000 copies in June 2000. And in its fourth launch, in Ahmedabad on 23 June 2003, it entered as number one with 452,000 copies - a world record...

http://www.dainikbhaskargroup.com/pdf/Media-Center-Case-Studies/Making-Breakthrough-Innovation.pdf

Chapter 7:

You should have got this right if you read the preface at the beginning of this book.

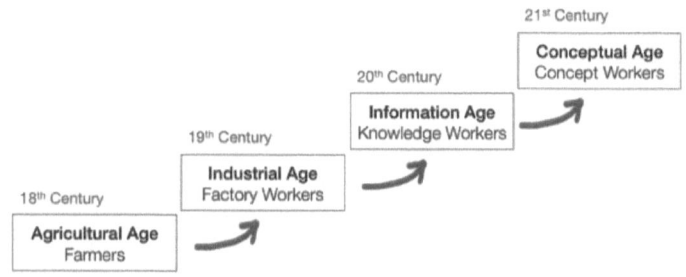

http://luizfirmino.blogspot.in/2012/03/look-forward-from-agricultural-age-to.html

Chapter 8:

There is no right or wrong answer for this one. If you got this far, you must have found something interesting/revolting, agreeable/disagreeable, right/wrong,... in this book. Here is your opportunity to share your opinion about the ideas presented in this book and earn your own social currency regardless of whether you liked the book or hated it. Go to **www.theinnovationimperative.org**

About the Authors

Ranga Shetty

https://in.linkedin.com/in/rangashetty

Three decades of work experience in the software industry in U.S. and India - building world-class engineering teams, driving product innovation, transforming engineering processes and developing leadership talent at large technology companies (HP, Cabletron, Intuit, Yahoo, Altisource) and an advanced technology startup (Cygsoft). Educational qualifications include two Master's degrees - one in Electrical Engineering from Rensselaer and another in Engineering Management from Stanford University.

ABOUT THE AUTHORS

Sajithra K

https://in.linkedin.com/in/sajithra

Sajithra K has 11+ years of experience (HP, Bell Labs, Alcatel-Lucent (Now Nokia), Altisource etc.) with cross functional expertise in Organizational Strategy, Marketing, Business Operations, and Employee Innovation. She has a Master's degree in Business Administration and a Bachelor's degree in Electronics and Communications Engineering. Sajithra K launched an ecommerce platform Officepooling.org under her startup Buzzmerize Business Solutions Pvt. Ltd in April'2016. Her book 'Trees from dirty seeds' is available on Amazon Kindle. Her paper on Social media is referenced by Authors worldwide, including US, UK, Turkey etc in papers, PhD thesis, and books.

www.ingramcontent.com/pod-product-compliance
Lightning Source LLC
Chambersburg PA
CBHW031439210526
45464CB00005B/2263